THE LITTLE CHEESE COOKBOOK

THE LITTLE CHEESE COOKBOOK

HERMES HOUSE

First published in the UK in 1998 by Hermes House

Hermes House is an imprint of
Anness Publishing Limited
Hermes House
88–89 Blackfriars Road
London SE1 8HA

ISBN 1-901289-60-5

Publisher Joanna Lorenz
Senior Cookery Editor Linda Fraser
Series Editor Sarah Ainley
Copy Editor Jenni Fleetwood
Designers Patrick McLeavey & Hannah Attwell
Illustrator Anna Koska
Photographers Edward Allwright, James Duncan, Michelle Garrett, Amanda Heywood, Patrick McLeavey, Michael Michaels & Don Last
Recipes Jacqueline Clark, Carole Clements, Roz Denny, Joanna Farrow, Christine France, Silvana Franco, Christine Ingram, Jenny Stacy, Steven Wheeler & Elizabeth Wolf-Cohen

For all recipes, quantities are given in both metric and imperial measures, and, where appropriate, measures are also given in standard cups and spoons. Follow one set, but not a mixture, because they are not interchangeable.

Printed and bound in China

1 3 5 7 9 10 8 6 4 2

Contents

Introduction

Say cheese and you can't help smiling. Few foods can claim the same degree of popularity. A cheese-lover can be any age, from the toddler blissfully nibbling a finger of Edam to the pensioner taking pleasure in a cheese scone. In many countries cheese appears on the breakfast table with fruit or sliced cold meats and, as every ploughman knows, it's the perfect partner for bread and pickles. For more formal occasions cheese appears in a number of guises, from simple soufflés or salads, through gratins, quiches and bakes to creamy cheesecakes.

Cheese happily takes centre stage as a fonduta or fondue or it can play a lesser but vital role as a topping. Cannelloni would certainly languish without cheese, and where would a pizza be without it?

From a nutritional point of view, cheese is an excellent protein food. The calcium it contributes to the diet builds healthy bones and teeth, and also helps to make muscles work efficiently. If the fat content in cheese causes you concern, remember that, as a rule, soft cheese is generally lower in fat than hard cheese. Or take advantage of the increasing number of reduced-fat varieties of soft and hard cheese that are available today.

The choice for vegetarians is also on the increase. The rennet used in conventional cheese production is of animal origin, but it is now possible to obtain some hard cheeses that are rennet-free.

Legend has it that cheese was first produced centuries ago, when an Asian nomad poured some milk into a bag made from an animal's stomach, tied it to his camel's saddle and set off on a day's trek across the desert. By the time he reached the next oasis, the movement of the camel, combined with the rennet still present in the bag, had caused the milk to separate into curds and whey.

Today the process is somewhat more sophisticated but the results remain the same. Milk (which can be full cream, semi-skimmed or skimmed) is heated, then treated with a starter culture which causes it to sour and separate. The curds are cut and drained – the degree of drainage depends on the desired result – and are then left to firm, naturally or by being compressed.

Of course, this is a simplification of what is an ancient art: great cheesemakers devote hours to perfecting the cheeses in their care. Factors such as temperature and humidity are carefully controlled, and how a cheese matures and ripens is a crucial part of the production process.

Although most hard cheeses are made from curds, the whey need not go to waste. Some cheeses, including ricotta, are made from whey, while varying amounts of whey are mixed with the curds of naturally soured milk or cream to make cottage cheese, curd cheese and cream cheese. Mild and moist, these cheeses can be low or high in fat, and must be eaten as soon as possible after purchase.

Whether you like it soft and creamy or prefer it strong and more mature, cheese is the favourite ingredient few of us would care to live without.

Types of Cheese

BAVARIAN SMOKED CHEESE
Sold in rounds, with a brown wax coating, Bavarian smoked cheese has a pale creamy colour and mild smoky flavour. It makes a good alternative topping for pizzas and jacket potatoes, and is excellent served or cooked with ham.

BRIE
France is the origin of this creamy cow's milk cheese, which is now readily available from supermarkets. The white, floury crust is edible. Look for plump, soft, but not runny cheese.

CAMEMBERT
Sold in rounds or wedges, Camembert is a creamy French cheese with a soft, smooth rind. It is very similar in appearance to Brie, although it has a more pronounced flavour.

CHEDDAR
Cheddar has a close texture and a colour that ranges from pale honey to deep gold. Depending on its maturity, the flavour can be mild or sharp and nutty. Cheddar is excellent for cooking as it melts without becoming stringy.

CHEVRE
Chèvre is the generic term for goat's milk cheeses. The texture varies from soft and moist to hard and dry, and the taste is usually quite tart. Soft varieties of goat's milk cheeses are usually moulded in cones or rolls. Goat's milk cheeses are commonly available from supermarkets.

EDAM
A ball-shaped, red-rinded cheese from Holland, Edam has a mild flavour. It is relatively low in fat and is often called the slimmer's cheese.

EMMENTHAL
A wonderful Swiss cooking cheese, Emmenthal is sweet and nutty, with distinctive grape-size holes.

FETA
A Greek cheese, traditionally made from sheep's milk. The lightly pressed curds have a fresh, tangy flavour. Feta is frequently stored in fresh or lightly salted water to keep it moist.

GORGONZOLA

This soft-textured blue cheese comes from Italy. The flavour ranges from mild to very sharp (Gorgonzola piccante). Gorgonzola is excellent sprinkled over pizza, and makes a wonderful base for a rich, cheesy pasta sauce.

GRUYERE

Gruyère is more moist than Emmenthal, which it resembles, and has a full, fruity flavour. This Swiss cheese retains its flavour when cooked and is perhaps most famously used in fondues.

MASCARPONE

A creamy full fat soft cheese that is often used in desserts, or served solo with fresh fruit. Mixed with natural yogurt, it makes a very good alternative to whipped cream.

MOZZARELLA

A moist, delicately flavoured soft cheese. Mozzarella was originally made from the milk of water buffaloes, but is now more commonly made with cow's milk. Eat mozzarella as soon as possible after purchase to enjoy it at its best.

PARMESAN

Italy's gift to the cook, this hard cheese has a wonderfully distinctive flavour. Buy it in the piece and grate it as needed, as the flavour of prepacked grated cheese is often disappointing.

RICOTTA

A fresh full fat whey cheese, ricotta has a mild, slightly sweet flavour. Ricotta is often used in desserts and makes an excellent cheesecake.

ROQUEFORT

A famous French crumbly blue-veined cheese traditionally made from sheep's milk, Roquefort tastes best when fully mature.

Techniques

GRATING

Choose a metal grater with a variety of grating surfaces with holes of different sizes. Square, triangular or hexagonal graters are easy to use, especially if there is a handle to prevent you from grating your fingers. Always use a firm, even pressure.

SLICING

Some cheeses, such as mozzarella, are better sliced than grated. Use a knife with a sharp, wide blade, and don't make the slices too thin. To pare Parmesan for garnishing, use a cheese slice or potato peeler.

MELTING

The secret of melting cheese successfully is to use a low temperature. Too high a heat may cause the cheese to curdle, separating into a blob of stringy curd surrounded by fat. It helps if you can melt the cheese with a liquid, such as wine or beer, but even then the heat should be low and the pan should be pulled off the heat as soon as the cheese has melted. Remove the pan from the heat, too, when adding grated cheese to a hot sauce, such as a white sauce, and avoid reheating it. Good cheeses for melting include Cheddar, Gruyère and Red Leicester (which gives a sauce a rich golden colour). Lancashire is a good toasting cheese, while fresh Parmesan makes a beautiful topping when melted on a gratin or pizza. Mix grated cheese with breadcrumbs for an even more successful result.

Champion Cheese Snacks

QUICK PIZZA SCONES

Cut fresh scones in half and spread the cut sides with red pesto. Top with a slice of tomato and dried oregano and season to taste. Sprinkle with grated Cheddar cheese and grill until golden and bubbling.

TOASTED ROLLS WITH CHEVRE

Cut bread rolls in half and toast the cut sides. Spread the rolls with home-made tomato sauce, sprinkle with snipped fresh basil and top with slices of chèvre (goat's cheese). Grill until the cheese melts.

CIABATTA WITH MOZZARELLA

Cut a loaf of ciabatta in half and toast the cut sides lightly. Spread with 60ml/4 tbsp red pesto or a mixture of tomato purée and mild red pepper mustard. Slice 2 small onions thickly, brush the slices lightly with olive oil and grill until lightly browned. Top the ciabatta with 225g/8oz sliced mozzarella cheese, arrange the onion slices on top and scatter over some black olives. Grill for about 2 minutes, until the cheese melts and the onion chars.

COOK'S TIP

Although cheeses are best bought in small quantities for immediate consumption, those with a high fat content (above 45 percent) can be frozen. Wrap cheeses carefully and thaw well before using them for cooking or eating.

Starters & Snacks

Egg & Cheese Soup

Ingredients

3 eggs
45ml/3 tbsp fine semolina
90ml/6 tbsp freshly grated Parmesan cheese
pinch of grated nutmeg
1.5 litres/2½ pints/6 cups cold beef or chicken stock
salt and ground black pepper
12 rounds of French bread, to serve

Serves 6

1 Mix the eggs, semolina and Parmesan in a bowl. Beat the mixture lightly, then add the nutmeg. Gradually beat in 250ml/8fl oz/1 cup of the cold stock. Meanwhile, bring the remaining stock to simmering point in a large saucepan.

2 When you are almost ready to serve the soup, whisk the egg mixture again, then pour it into the simmering stock, whisking all the time. Raise the heat slightly and bring the mixture to just below boiling point.

3 Season the soup with salt and ground black pepper. Cook for 3–4 minutes, whisking gently. As the egg cooks, the soup should begin to take on a slightly grainy appearance.

4 Toast the rounds of French bread under the grill and place two rounds in the bottom of each soup plate. Ladle the hot soup over and serve at once.

Cook's Tip

Home-made beef or chicken stock – or broth – is best for this soup. Do not let it boil after adding the egg mixture.

Creole Cheese & Potato Puffs

INGREDIENTS

45ml/3 tbsp milk
25g/1oz/2 tbsp butter, plus extra for greasing
450g/1lb/2½ cups cold mashed potatoes
50g/2oz/½ cup grated mature Cheddar cheese
4 spring onions, finely chopped
grated nutmeg
salt and ground black pepper
2 eggs, separated
watercress and cherry tomatoes, to garnish

SERVES 4–6

1 Preheat the oven to 220°C/425°F/Gas 7. Generously grease a 12-hole non-stick bun tin, greasing the sections between the holes as well. Put the milk and measured butter in a small pan and bring to just below boiling point.

2 Pour the hot milk mixture into the mashed potatoes, mixing well, then stir in the cheese and spring onions, with salt, pepper and nutmeg to taste. Beat in the egg yolks.

3 Whisk the egg whites in a grease-free bowl to soft peaks. Mix a spoonful or two of the egg whites into the potato mixture to lighten it, then fold in the rest of the whites as lightly as you can.

4 Spoon the mixture into the bun tins. Bake for 15 minutes or until the puffs have risen and are golden brown. Serve at once, garnished with watercress and cherry tomatoes.

VARIATION

Instead of heating the butter with the milk, use it to fry the spring onions lightly. Stir in 10ml/2 tbsp good-quality curry powder and cook for 1 minute, then stir the mixture into the mashed potatoes after adding the milk. Continue as in the main recipe.

Roquefort & Cucumber Mousse

Ingredients

18cm/7in piece of cucumber
75ml/5 tbsp cold water
10ml/2 tsp powdered gelatine
90g/3½ oz/generous ½ cup Roquefort cheese, crumbled
200g/7oz/scant 1 cup full-fat soft cheese
45ml/3 tbsp crème fraîche
cayenne pepper
seedless red and green grapes and mint leaves, to garnish

Serves 6

1 Cut the cucumber lengthways into quarters. Remove the peel and seeds, then dice the flesh. Put the water in a small bowl and sprinkle the gelatine on top. Leave until spongy, then place over simmering water. Stir until the gelatine has dissolved completely.

2 Process the Roquefort, soft cheese and crème fraîche in a food processor until smooth. Add the gelatine mixture and process to mix, then add the cucumber and pulse until it is finely chopped but not puréed. Season with cayenne.

3 Rinse a 1 litre/1¾ pint/4 cup mould with cold water. Spoon in the mixture, level the surface and chill for 4–6 hours, until set.

4 To turn out, run a knife around the edge of the mould, dip it in hot water briefly, then invert a plate over the top. Turn over the plate and mould and shake firmly to release the mousse. Garnish with the red and green grapes and mint leaves.

Twice-baked Cheese Soufflés

INGREDIENTS

20g/¾oz/1½ tbsp butter, plus extra for greasing
30ml/2 tbsp plain flour
150ml/¼ pint/⅔ cup milk
1 small bay leaf
2 eggs, separated, plus 1 egg white, at room temperature
75g/3oz/¾ cup grated Gruyère cheese
1.5ml/¼ tsp cream of tartar
salt and ground black pepper
grated nutmeg
TOMATO CREAM SAUCE
300ml/½ pint/1¼ cups whipping cream
10ml/2 tsp tomato purée
1 ripe tomato, peeled, seeded and finely diced
salt and cayenne pepper

SERVES 6

1 Preheat the oven to 190°C/375°F/Gas 5. Generously grease six individual ramekins; line the base of each with non-stick baking paper.

2 Melt the butter in a saucepan, sift in the flour and cook until pale golden in colour, stirring all the time. Gradually add the milk, whisking until the mixture boils and thickens. Add the bay leaf, with salt, pepper and nutmeg to taste. Lower the heat and simmer for 1 minute more, stirring.

3 Remove the white sauce from the heat, take out the bay leaf and beat in the egg yolks, one at a time. Finally stir in the cheese until it has melted and the mixture is smooth. Set aside.

4 Whisk the egg whites in a grease-free bowl until frothy, then add the cream of tartar and beat until they form soft peaks. Whisk a spoonful of the egg whites into the cheese sauce to lighten it, then fold in the remainder.

5 Divide the mixture among the ramekins, filling them about three-quarters full. Put the ramekins in a roasting tin and pour in boiling water to come halfway up the sides of the dishes. Bake for about 18 minutes, until the soufflés are puffy and golden brown. Allow them to cool in the dishes until they deflate. Leave the oven on.

6 Meanwhile, make the sauce. Bring the cream just to the boil in a small saucepan. Lower the heat, stir in the tomato purée and diced tomato and cook for 2–3 minutes. Season with salt and cayenne. Spoon a layer of sauce into a gratin dish just large enough to hold the soufflés. Run a knife around each soufflé and invert it in the dish. Lift off the lining paper, pour the remaining sauce over and bake the soufflés for 12–15 minutes until well browned.

Farine

Fried Mozzarella

INGREDIENTS

350g/12oz mozzarella cheese, in the piece
flour seasoned with salt and ground black pepper
2 eggs
plain dry breadcrumbs
oil, for deep frying
fresh herb sprigs, to garnish

SERVES 2–3

1 Cut the mozzarella into 1cm/½in slices. Gently pat off the excess moisture with kitchen paper. Spread out the seasoned flour in a shallow bowl, beat the eggs in another, and sprinkle the breadcrumbs over a sheet of foil.

2 Heat the oil to a temperature of 185°C/360°F or until a small piece of bread sizzles as soon as it is dropped in. Press the cheese slices into the flour to coat them thinly and evenly. Dip them in the egg, then coat them in the breadcrumbs, pressing the crumbs on firmly all over.

3 Fry the coated mozzarella rounds in the hot oil until golden brown. Do this in batches if you must, but do not let the coated cheese stand for too long before frying or the breadcrumbs will separate from the cheese during frying. Drain on kitchen paper and serve hot with a herb garnish.

COOK'S TIP

Serve the cheese Italian-style, with a freshly cooked tomato and basil sauce, or with a tart cranberry or redcurrant sauce for a contemporary flavour.

Cheese Scones

INGREDIENTS

225g/8oz/2 cups plain flour
12ml/2½ tsp baking powder
2.5ml/½ tsp mustard powder
2.5ml/½ tsp salt
50g/2oz/¼ cup butter, diced
75g/3oz/¾ cup grated Cheddar cheese
150ml/¼ pint/⅔ cup milk, plus extra for glazing
1 egg, beaten

MAKES 12

1 Preheat the oven to 230°C/450°F/Gas 8. Gently sift the flour, baking powder, mustard powder and salt into a mixing bowl. Rub in the butter until the mixture resembles breadcrumbs, then stir in two-thirds of the grated cheese.

2 Make a well in the centre of the flour mixture and add the milk and egg. Mix quickly to a dough, then turn out on to a lightly floured surface.

3 Roll out the dough lightly, or simply pat it out. Cut into squares, triangles or rounds. Brush lightly with milk and sprinkle with the remaining cheese. Leave to stand for 15 minutes, then place on a baking sheet and bake for 15 minutes or until well risen and golden. Serve the scones warm.

COOK'S TIP

The secret of good scones is to handle the dough lightly, bake at a high temperature and serve freshly cooked. For a special starter, top with cream cheese and strips of smoked salmon.

Cheesy Quesadillas

INGREDIENTS

275g/10oz/2 cups masa harina (tortilla flour)
250–350ml/8–12fl oz/1–1½ cups water
oil, for frying
finely shredded lettuce, to garnish
FILLING
225g/8oz/1 cup finely chopped or grated mature Cheddar cheese
3 jalapeño chillies, seeded and cut into strips
salt

MAKES 14

1 In a bowl, mix the masa harina with 250ml/8fl oz/1 cup of the water to make a dough that just holds together. Add a little more water if necessary. Cover and set aside for 15 minutes.

2 Lightly knead the dough, then shape it into 14 balls. Using a tortilla press, make 14 tortillas. Make the filling by mixing the cheese and chillies together in a bowl. Season with salt.

3 Heat the oil in a large frying pan. Holding an unbaked tortilla on your palm, put a spoonful of filling along the centre, avoiding the edges.

4 Fold the tortilla over the filling and seal the edges by pressing or crimping them together. Make more quesadillas in the same way, frying them in batches in the hot oil until they are golden brown and crisp.

5 Drain the cooked quesadillas on kitchen paper and serve them hot, with a garnish of finely shredded lettuce.

COOK'S TIP

If you line both sides of the tortilla press with clear film or polythene, you will find it easier to handle the tortillas.

Welsh Rarebit

Ingredients

115g/4oz/1 cup grated mature Cheddar cheese
30ml/2 tbsp brown ale
5ml/1 tsp prepared English mustard
cayenne pepper
4 slices of bread

Makes 4

1 Put the grated Cheddar cheese in a saucepan. Pour in the brown ale, then add the mustard, with cayenne to taste. Stir until well mixed, then heat gently, stirring all the time until the cheese begins to melt.

2 Toast the slices of bread on one side under a medium grill, then turn the slices over and toast the second side lightly. Spoon the cheese mixture over the toasts, spreading it all the way to the edges.

3 Slide the grill pan back under the heat and grill the toasts until the cheese topping is golden and beginning to brown. Serve at once.

Variations

Although brown ale (beer) is usually used to make Welsh rarebit, you can use red wine to vary the flavour. Any hard cheese is suitable, so try Red Leicester for a change, or use a mixture of Cheddar and Stilton. If you serve a poached egg on top, the dish becomes a Buck Rarebit.

Cheese & Ham Croissants

INGREDIENTS

4 large croissants
50g/2oz/¼ cup butter, softened
4 slices of Bayonne or Parma ham
115–175g/4–6oz rinded Camembert or Brie, sliced about 5mm/¼in thick
Dijon mustard
lettuce, tomatoes and chives, to serve

SERVES 4

1 Preheat the oven to 200°C/400°F/Gas 6. Split the croissants lengthways and spread each side with butter and a little mustard.

2 Place a slice of the cured ham on the bottom half of each croissant, trimming it to fit. Arrange slices of cheese on the ham and cover with the croissant tops.

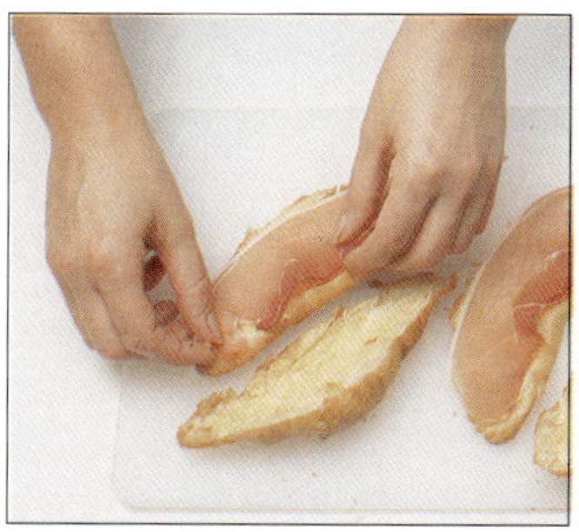

3 Place the croissants on a baking sheet. Cover them lightly with foil, then bake for 3–5 minutes, until the cheese starts to melt. Serve at once, with lettuce, tomatoes and chives.

COOK'S TIP

For an everyday snack, use honey-baked ham and Gruyère or even Cheddar cheese. Experiment with different mustards – a mild red pepper mustard is particularly good.

Main Meals

Cheeseburgers

INGREDIENTS

50g/2oz/⅓ cup bulgur wheat
225g/8oz minced beef
1 onion, finely chopped
15ml/1 tbsp finely chopped fresh parsley
15ml/1 tbsp tomato purée
15ml/1 tbsp freshly grated Parmesan cheese
1 egg, beaten
4 burger buns
lettuce leaves
4 cheese slices
salt and ground black pepper
tomato relish, to serve (optional)

SERVES 4

1 Place the bulgur wheat in a bowl and add boiling water to cover. Leave to stand for 10 minutes, then drain off any liquid that has not been absorbed.

2 Put the minced beef in a bowl and break it up with a fork. Add the onion, parsley, then the tomato purée and Parmesan. Add the bulgur wheat and mix well, first with a fork and then with clean hands.

3 Stir in enough of the beaten egg to bind the mixture. Divide it into four portions and shape each into a burger. Grill under a medium heat for 8–10 minutes on each side until cooked through.

4 Meanwhile, split the burger buns in half and toast under the grill for 1 minute. Place one or two lettuce leaves on the bottom half of each bun. Add a burger and top with a cheese slice. Season to taste with salt and pepper, then replace the bun lid or set it to one side. Serve the cheeseburgers with chips and a spoonful of tomato relish, if liked.

Pizza with Four Cheeses

INGREDIENTS

175g/6oz/1½ cups strong white flour
1.5ml/¼ tsp salt
5ml/1 tsp easy-blend dried yeast
15ml/1 tbsp olive oil
about 150ml/¼ pint/⅔ cup hand-hot water
TOPPING
75g/3oz/½ cup Gorgonzola or other blue cheese, thinly sliced
75g/3oz/½ cup mozzarella cheese, finely diced
75g/3oz/½ cup chèvre (goat's cheese), thinly sliced
75g/3oz/¾ cup mature Cheddar cheese, coarsely grated
4 fresh sage leaves, torn
45ml/3 tbsp olive oil

SERVES 4

1 Sift the flour and salt into a large mixing bowl. Stir in the yeast. Make a well in the centre and add the olive oil, with enough of the hand-hot water to make a soft, malleable dough.

2 Knead the dough on a lightly floured surface for 10 minutes, until smooth and elastic, then return to the clean bowl, cover with clear film and leave in a warm place for 1 hour, until doubled in bulk.

3 Preheat the oven to 220°C/425°F/Gas 7. Turn the dough on to a lightly floured surface and knead again for 2–3 minutes. Roll out to a 30cm/12in round and place on a large baking sheet. Push up the dough edges to make a rim.

4 Lightly score the pizza into quarters. Arrange the blue cheese on one quarter wedge and the mozzarella on another, then fill the remaining wedges with goat's cheese and grated Cheddar.

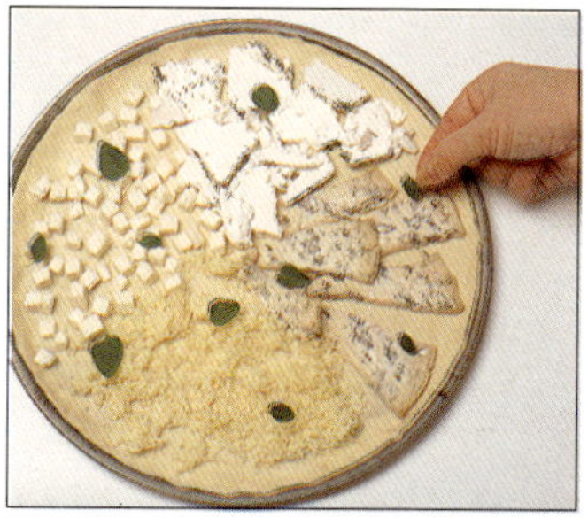

5 Scatter sage leaves over the top of the pizza and drizzle with the olive oil. Bake for 20 minutes, until the crust is golden brown and the cheese topping is bubbling.

Parmesan Chicken

INGREDIENTS

4 boneless, skinless chicken breasts
25g/1oz/¼ cup plain flour
olive oil, for frying
225g/8oz/1½ cups mozzarella cheese, sliced
60ml/4 tbsp freshly grated Parmesan cheese
30ml/2 tbsp fresh white breadcrumbs
salt and ground black pepper
TOMATO SAUCE
15ml/1 tbsp olive oil
1 onion, finely chopped
1 celery stick, finely chopped
1 red pepper, seeded and diced
1 garlic clove, crushed
400g/14oz can chopped tomatoes with basil
150ml/¼ pint/⅔ cup chicken stock
15ml/1 tbsp tomato purée
10ml/2 tsp caster sugar

SERVES 4

1 Make the tomato sauce. Heat the oil in a large frying pan and fry the onion, celery and pepper until tender. Stir in the remaining ingredients. Bring to the boil, lower the heat and simmer for 30 minutes, stirring occasionally.

2 Divide each chicken breast into two fillets, place between sheets of clear film and flatten with a rolling pin. Spread out the flour in a shallow dish. Season the flour, then coat the chicken. Preheat the oven to 180°C/350°F/Gas 4.

3 Heat the olive oil for frying in a large frying pan. Cook the chicken escalopes quickly in batches for 3–4 minutes until coloured. Drain on kitchen paper. Spread half the tomato sauce in a large baking dish. Add the escalopes, spoon the rest of the sauce over and top with the mozzarella.

4 Mix the Parmesan cheese with the breadcrumbs and sprinkle over the mozzarella. Bake for 20–30 minutes, until the topping is golden brown.

Chicken with Ham & Cheese

INGREDIENTS

4 small skinless, boneless chicken breasts
flour seasoned with salt and ground black pepper
50g/2oz/¼ cup butter
3–4 fresh sage leaves
4 thin slices of prosciutto crudo or cooked ham, cut in half
50g/2oz/⅔ cup freshly grated Parmesan cheese
fresh sage sprigs, to garnish

SERVES 4

1 Cut each chicken breast in half lengthways to make two fillets of about the same thickness. Spread out the seasoned flour in a shallow dish. Lightly coat the chicken pieces, shaking off any excess flour.

2 Heat the butter in a large heavy frying pan. Add the sage leaves and then the chicken pieces, arranging them in a single layer. Cook over a low to medium heat for about 15 minutes, until the chicken is golden on both sides. Preheat the grill.

3 Use a fish slice to transfer the chicken pieces to a rack placed over the grill pan. Place a piece of ham on each chicken fillet, then top with the grated Parmesan. Grill for 3–4 minutes, or until the cheese has melted. Serve at once, with a garnish of fresh sage.

VARIATION

Before topping each chicken breast with ham and cheese, spread lightly with red pesto. Garnish with lightly grilled cherry tomatoes.

Ham & Cheese Veal Escalopes

INGREDIENTS

8 veal escalopes, total weight about 450g/1lb, preferably cut across the grain
plain flour, seasoned with salt and ground black pepper
25g/1oz/2 tbsp butter
30ml/2 tbsp olive oil
45ml/3 tbsp dry white wine
8 small slices of cooked ham
50g/2oz/⅔ cup freshly grated Parmesan cheese, or 8 small slices of Gruyère cheese
fresh parsley, to garnish

SERVES 4

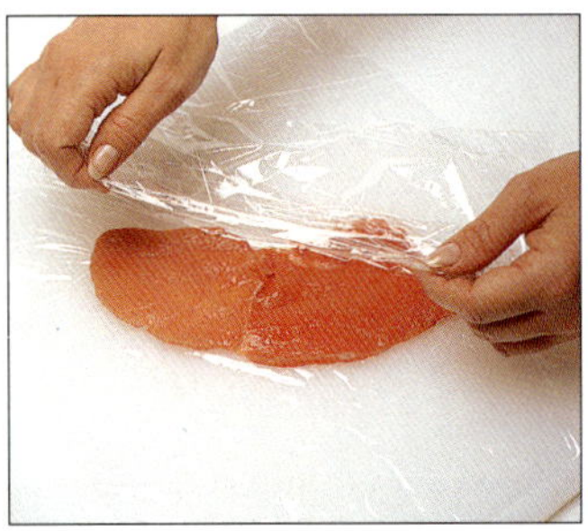

1 Preheat the oven to 200°C/400°F/Gas 6. Place each veal escalope in turn between sheets of clear film and flatten with a rolling pin. If they have not been cut across the grain, snip the edges at intervals to stop them from curling up during cooking.

2 Spread the seasoned flour in a large shallow dish. Heat the butter and oil in a large frying pan. Lightly coat the veal slices in the flour, shaking off any excess. In batches, brown them quickly on both sides in the butter mixture, then arrange them in a single layer in a shallow baking dish.

3 Add the wine to the frying pan and cook for 1–2 minutes, scraping in any sediment on the bottom of the pan. Pour over the escalopes, then place a small slice of ham on each. Sprinkle with Parmesan or top each escalope with a slice of Gruyère cheese. Bake for 5–7 minutes, or until the cheese melts. Garnish with the fresh parsley and serve.

Pasta with Prawns & Feta

INGREDIENTS

450g/1lb raw prawns
6 spring onions
50g/2oz/¼ cup butter
225g/8oz feta cheese, cut into 1cm/½in cubes
small bunch of fresh chives, snipped
450g/1lb/4 cups dried penne or other pasta shapes
salt and ground black pepper

SERVES 4

1 To remove the heads from the prawns, twist them firmly and pull off. Peel and devein the prawns, discarding the shells. Chop the spring onions finely.

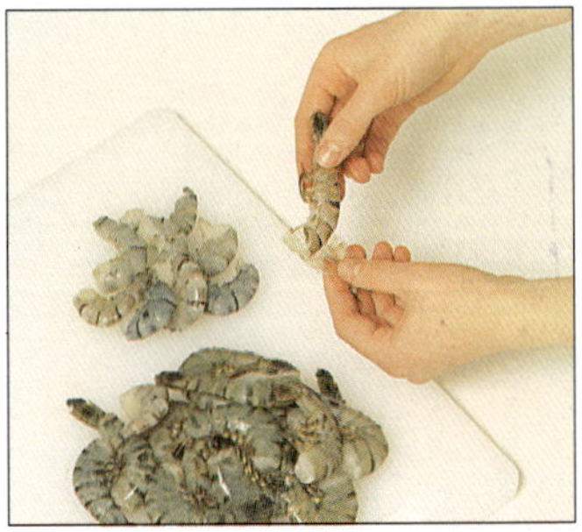

2 Melt the butter in a frying pan and stir in the prawns. As soon as they turn pink, add the spring onions and cook gently for 1 minute.

3 Stir the feta cubes into the prawn mixture. Season with black pepper. Stir in half the chives and set the rest aside for the garnish.

4 Meanwhile, bring a large saucepan of lightly salted water to the boil. Add the pasta and cook for 10 minutes or according to the instructions on the packet, until it is just tender. Drain well, pile into a heated serving dish and top with the sauce. Scatter the reserved chives over and serve.

COOK'S TIP

Look out for feta cubes in oil. Available in jars, they are ideal for this recipe.

Penne with Tuna & Mozzarella

INGREDIENTS

450g/1lb/4 cups dried penne or other pasta shapes
15ml/1 tbsp drained bottled capers
2 garlic cloves
45ml/3 tbsp chopped fresh parsley
200g/7oz can tuna, drained
75ml/5 tbsp olive oil
115g/4oz/⅔ cup mozzarella cheese, diced
salt and ground black pepper

SERVES 4

1 Bring a large saucepan of lightly salted water to the boil. Add the pasta and cook for 10–12 minutes or according to the instructions on the packet, until it is just tender.

2 Meanwhile, chop the capers finely with the garlic. Scrape the mixture into a bowl and add the chopped fresh parsley and tuna. Stir in the oil. Season with salt and ground black pepper, if necessary.

3 Drain the pasta and tip it into a large frying pan. Add the tuna sauce and the diced mozzarella. Cook over a medium heat, stirring all the time, until the cheese begins to melt. Serve at once.

Cannelloni

INGREDIENTS

8 dried cannelloni tubes
115g/4oz spinach leaves, trimmed
FILLING
15ml/1 tbsp sunflower oil
175g/6oz minced beef
2 garlic cloves, crushed
30ml/2 tbsp plain flour
120ml/4fl oz/½ cup beef stock
1 small carrot, finely chopped
1 small yellow courgette, chopped
salt and ground black pepper
SAUCE
25g/1oz/2 tbsp butter
15g/½oz/2 tbsp plain flour
250ml/8fl oz/1 cup milk
50g/2oz/½ cup freshly grated
Parmesan cheese

SERVES 4

1 Preheat the oven to 180°C/350°F/Gas 4. Make the filling. Heat the oil in a large saucepan, add the minced beef and break it up with a spoon. Stir in the garlic and cook for 5 minutes.

2 Stir in the flour and cook for 1 minute more. Add the stock, stirring all the time, and bring to the boil. Add the chopped carrot and courgette, with plenty of salt and pepper. Cook for 10 minutes.

3 Spoon the filling into the cannelloni tubes and arrange them in a single layer in a baking dish. Bring a small saucepan of water to the boil, blanch the spinach leaves for 3 minutes, then drain them well and arrange on top of the cannelloni.

4 Make the sauce. Melt the butter in a saucepan. Stir in the flour and cook for 1 minute. Gradually add the milk, stirring until the mixture boils and thickens. Add the cheese and stir over the heat until it melts.

5 Pour the sauce over the cannelloni and spinach. Bake for 30 minutes or until the topping is golden. Serve with tomatoes and a mixed leaf salad.

Vegetarian Dishes

Fonduta

INGREDIENTS

250g/9oz fontina or Gruyère cheese, diced
250ml/8fl oz/1 cup creamy milk
15g/½oz/1 tbsp butter
2 eggs, lightly beaten
ground black pepper
warm ciabatta or focaccia, cubed, to serve

SERVES 4

1 Put the diced fontina or Gruyère cheese in a bowl. Pour over the milk, cover and leave to soak for 2–3 hours. Tip into the top of a double boiler or a heat-proof bowl which will fit snugly over a saucepan.

2 Add the butter and eggs to the cheese mixture. Cook over barely simmering water, stirring constantly, until the cheese has melted to make a smooth sauce with the consistency of custard.

3 Remove the saucepan or bowl from the heat and season the fonduta with pepper. Transfer to a serving dish, grind some pepper over and serve at once, with the warm bread cubes for dipping.

COOK'S TIP

Do not overheat the sauce, or it may curdle. A very gentle heat will produce a lovely smooth sauce. If possible, keep it warm over a candle at the table.

Baked Cheese Polenta with Tomato Sauce

INGREDIENTS

1 litre/1¾ pints/4 cups water
5ml/1 tsp salt
250g/9oz/2¼ cups quick-cook polenta
5ml/1 tsp paprika
2.5ml/½ tsp grated nutmeg
30ml/2 tbsp olive oil
1 large onion, finely chopped
2 garlic cloves, crushed
2 x 400g/14oz cans chopped tomatoes
15ml/1 tbsp tomato purée
5ml/1 tsp sugar
75g/3oz/¾ cup grated Gruyère cheese
salt and ground black pepper

SERVES 4

1 Preheat the oven to 200°C/400°F/Gas 6. Line a 28 x 18cm/11 x 7in baking tin with clear film. Bring the water to the boil, stir in the salt, then add the polenta in a steady stream. Cook, stirring all the time, for 5 minutes.

2 Beat the paprika and nutmeg into the polenta, then pour it into the prepared tin. Smooth the surface and set aside to cool and become firm.

3 Heat the oil in a large frying pan and cook the onion and garlic over a gentle heat for 10 minutes, until softened. Stir in the tomatoes, tomato purée and sugar, with salt and pepper to taste. Bring to the boil, lower the heat and simmer for 20 minutes.

4 Turn the cold polenta out on to a board. Cut into 5cm/2in squares. Place half the squares in a greased baking dish. Spoon over half the tomato sauce, then sprinkle over half the cheese. Repeat the layers. Bake for 25 minutes, until golden.

Risotto with Parmesan

Ingredients

1.2 litres/2 pints/5 cups vegetable stock, preferably home-made
65g/2½oz/5 tbsp butter
1 small onion, finely chopped
275g/10oz/1½ cups risotto rice
120ml/4fl oz/½ cup dry white wine
75g/3oz/¾ cup freshly grated Parmesan cheese
salt and ground black pepper

Serves 3–4

1 Bring the stock to the boil in a large saucepan. Lower the heat so that it barely simmers and have a ladle handy.

2 Melt two-thirds of the butter in a large heavy-based frying pan. Stir in the onion and cook gently until it is soft and golden. Add the rice, stirring to coat all the grains in butter. Cook for 1–2 minutes, then pour in the wine.

3 Raise the heat slightly and cook until the wine evaporates. Add a ladleful of hot stock and cook over a medium heat until it has been absorbed, stirring the rice with a wooden spoon to prevent it from sticking to the pan. Continue adding the stock in the same way, waiting until each ladleful has been absorbed before adding the next.

4 After about 30 minutes, when all the stock has been added, and the rice is tender and creamy, switch off the heat and stir in the remaining butter and the Parmesan. Season the risotto with salt and pepper to taste. Set it aside for 3–4 minutes before serving.

Spinach & Ricotta Gnocchi

INGREDIENTS

900g/2lb spinach leaves, washed and trimmed
350g/12oz/1½ cups ricotta cheese
60ml/4 tbsp freshly grated Parmesan cheese, plus extra to serve
3 eggs, beaten
1.5ml/¼ tsp grated nutmeg
45–60ml/3–4 tbsp plain flour
115g/4oz/½ cup butter, melted
salt and ground black pepper

SERVES 4

1 Place the spinach in a large shallow saucepan, with just the water that clings to the leaves after washing. Cook for about 5 minutes, until the spinach leaves are wilted. Drain in a colander, cool, then squeeze out as much liquid as possible. Process in a blender or food processor, then tip into a bowl.

2 Add the ricotta, Parmesan, eggs and nutmeg, with salt and pepper to taste. Mix well, adding enough of the flour to form a soft dough. Using clean hands, shape the mixture into 7.5cm/3in sausages, then dust lightly with flour.

3 Bring a large saucepan of lightly salted water to the boil. Gently slide the gnocchi into the water and cook for 1–2 minutes, until they float to the surface. Lift out the gnocchi with a slotted spoon and transfer them to a heated dish. Pour over the melted butter, sprinkle with Parmesan and serve.

Gorgonzola, Cauliflower & Walnut Gratin

Ingredients

1 large cauliflower, broken into florets
25g/1oz/2 tbsp butter
1 onion, finely chopped
45ml/3 tbsp plain flour
450ml/¾ pint/scant 2 cups milk
150g/5oz/scant 1 cup Gorgonzola or other blue cheese, cut into pieces
2.5ml/½ tsp celery salt
pinch of cayenne pepper
75g/3oz/¾ cup chopped walnuts
pinch of salt
fresh parsley, to garnish

Serves 4

1 Bring a large saucepan of lightly salted water to the boil. Add the cauliflower florets and cook for 6 minutes or until the florets are just tender. Drain the cauliflower and place it in a flameproof gratin dish.

2 Heat the butter in a heavy-based saucepan. Add the onion and cook over a gentle heat for 8 minutes until softened but not coloured. Stir in the flour and cook for 1 minute, then remove the pan from the heat and gradually add the milk, stirring constantly.

3 Return the pan to the heat and bring the sauce to the boil, stirring all the time, until the sauce thickens. Stir in the Gorgonzola or blue cheese, celery salt and cayenne pepper. Remove the pan from the heat.

4 Preheat the grill. Spoon the sauce over the cauliflower, scatter the chopped walnuts over and grill until golden. Garnish with the fresh parsley and serve at once.

Variations

Use broccoli or boiled celeriac instead of cauliflower, or use a mixture. The blue cheese sauce is also delicious served with pasta – sprinkle with some crumbled grilled bacon if making the dish for non-vegetarians.

Baked Tortellini with Three Cheeses

INGREDIENTS

25g/1oz/2 tbsp butter
450g/1lb/4 cups fresh tortellini
2 eggs
350g/12oz/1½ cups ricotta or curd cheese
handful of fresh basil leaves
115g/4oz smoked mozzarella cheese, sliced
60ml/4 tbsp freshly grated Parmesan cheese
salt and ground black pepper
fresh basil sprig, to garnish

SERVES 4

1 Preheat the oven to 190°C/375°F/Gas 5. Grease a baking dish with the butter. Bring a large saucepan of lightly salted water to the boil and add the tortellini. Cook according to the instructions on the packet, until just tender. Drain well.

2 Beat the eggs with the ricotta or curd cheese in a bowl. Add salt and pepper to taste. Spoon half the drained tortellini into the dish, pour over half the ricotta mixture, then scatter half the basil leaves on top.

3 Cover with the smoked mozzarella and the remaining basil. Spoon the rest of the tortellini on top and cover with the remaining ricotta mixture, spreading it level.

4 Sprinkle the Parmesan evenly over the surface. Bake for 35–45 minutes or until the topping is golden brown and bubbling. Serve at once, garnished with the basil sprig.

VARIATION

If smoked mozzarella is not available, use grated Bavarian smoked cheese instead.

Baked Macaroni with Cheese

INGREDIENTS

175g/6oz/2 cups grated Parmesan cheese or
175g/6oz/1½ cups grated Cheddar cheese
40g/1½oz/¾ cup fresh white breadcrumbs
450g/1lb/4 cups short-cut macaroni or other dried hollow pasta shapes
flat leaf parsley, to garnish
BECHAMEL SAUCE
475ml/16fl oz/2 cups milk
1 bay leaf
3 mace blades
50g/2oz/¼ cup butter
40g/1½oz/6 tbsp plain flour

SERVES 6

1 Make the béchamel sauce. In a small saucepan, heat the milk with the bay leaf and mace until just below boiling point. Set aside to infuse for about 30 minutes, then strain.

2 Melt the butter in a saucepan, stir in the flour and cook for 1 minute. Gradually add the flavoured milk, stirring constantly until the sauce boils and thickens. Remove the béchamel sauce from the heat, stir in three-quarters of the cheese, cover with the lid and set the pan aside.

3 Preheat the oven to 200°C/400°F/Gas 6. Grease an baking dish and sprinkle with half the breadcrumbs. Bring a large saucepan of lightly salted water to the boil. Add the pasta to the saucepan and cook for 7 minutes or according to the instructions on the packet.

4 When the pasta is just tender, drain it well and return it to the clean pan. Reheat the sauce, add it to the pasta and mix well. Spoon into the prepared dish, sprinkle with the rest of the grated cheese and remaining breadcrumbs and bake for 20 minutes. Garnish with flat leaf parsley and serve.

Vegetables & Salads

Baked Fennel with Parmesan

INGREDIENTS

1kg/2¼lb fennel bulbs
50g/2oz/¼ cup butter, plus extra for greasing
40g/1½oz/½ cup freshly grated Parmesan cheese
salt

SERVES 4–6

1 Preheat the oven to 200°C/400°F/Gas 6. Grease a large shallow baking dish. Bring a large saucepan of lightly salted water to the boil.

2 Use a sharp knife to trim the fennel bulbs, then cut them in half and add them to the saucepan of boiling water. Cook until the fennel is just tender, then drain.

3 Cut the fennel halves lengthways into four or six pieces. Arrange the pieces in a single layer in the baking dish. Dot them with the butter, then sprinkle the grated Parmesan evenly over the top. Bake in the oven for about 20 minutes, or until the topping is golden brown. Serve at once.

Cauliflower Cheese

Ingredients

1 large cauliflower, about 450g/1lb, broken into florets
40g/1½oz/3 tbsp butter, plus extra for greasing
40g/1½oz/6 tbsp plain flour
350ml/12fl oz/1½ cups milk
1 bay leaf
pinch of grated nutmeg
15ml/1 tbsp Dijon mustard
175g/6oz/1½ cups grated Gruyère or Emmenthal cheese
salt and ground black pepper

Serves 4–6

1 Preheat the oven to 180°C/350°F/Gas 4. Grease a large gratin dish or shallow baking dish.

2 Bring a large saucepan of lightly salted water to the boil, add the cauliflower florets and cook for 6–8 minutes until just tender.

3 Meanwhile, melt the butter in a heavy-based saucepan. Stir in the flour and cook for 1 minute, then gradually add the milk, stirring constantly until the sauce boils.

4 Add the bay leaf and season with salt, pepper and nutmeg. Lower the heat and simmer, stirring occasionally, for 5 minutes. Remove the pan from the heat, discard the bay leaf and stir in the mustard. Add half the cheese and stir until melted.

5 Drain the cauliflower well and arrange it in the dish. Pour over the cheese sauce and sprinkle the rest of the cheese on top. Bake for about 20 minutes or until the topping is bubbling and well browned.

Leeks with Ham & Cheese Sauce

INGREDIENTS

4 leeks, cleaned
4 slices of cooked ham
SAUCE
25g/1oz/2 tbsp butter
25g/1oz/¼ cup plain flour
300ml/½ pint/1¼ cups milk
2.5ml/½ tsp Dijon mustard
115g/4oz/1 cup grated mature Cheddar cheese
salt and ground black pepper

SERVES 4

1 Preheat the oven to 190°C/375°F/ Gas 5. Trim the leeks to within 2.5cm/1in of the white. Bring a large saucepan of lightly salted water to the boil, add the leeks and cook for about 20 minutes or until tender.

2 Meanwhile, make the sauce. Melt the butter in a heavy-based saucepan. Stir in the flour and cook for 1 minute, then gradually add the milk, stirring constantly until the sauce boils and thickens.

3 Remove the sauce from the heat and stir in the mustard, with three-quarters of the cheese. Add salt and freshly ground black pepper to taste.

4 Drain the leeks, lay them in an ovenproof dish, wrap them in the ham and coat them with the cheese sauce. Scatter the remaining cheese over the top and bake in the preheated oven for 20 minutes.

Aubergines Baked with Cheese

INGREDIENTS

1kg/2¼lb aubergines
plain flour, for coating
oil, for frying
40g/1½oz/½ cup freshly grated Parmesan cheese
450g/1lb/2½ cups mozzarella cheese, thinly sliced
olive oil, for drizzling
salt and ground black pepper
TOMATO SAUCE
60ml/4 tbsp olive oil
1 onion, very finely chopped
1 garlic clove, crushed
400g/14oz can chopped tomatoes with herbs

SERVES 4–6

1 Cut the aubergines into 1cm/½in rounds and layer them in a colander, sprinkling salt between the layers. Leave to drain for 1 hour.

2 Meanwhile, make the tomato sauce. Heat the oil in a saucepan and fry the onion for 5–8 minutes over a medium heat, until it is translucent. Stir in the garlic and tomatoes, with salt and pepper to taste. Bring the sauce to the boil, lower the heat and simmer for about 20 minutes, then purée in a blender or food processor.

3 Preheat the oven to 180°C/350°F/Gas 4. Rinse the aubergine slices and dry them on kitchen paper. Coat them lightly in flour. Heat the oil in a large frying pan, then fry them in batches until golden brown and tender. Drain each batch on kitchen paper while frying the next.

4 Grease a baking dish. Spread a little of the tomato sauce on the bottom, cover with a layer of aubergine slices and sprinkle with grated Parmesan. Season well and add a layer of mozzarella and a little more tomato sauce. Repeat the layers until all the ingredients have been used, ending with tomato sauce and a sprinkling of Parmesan. Drizzle a little olive oil over and bake in the oven for 45 minutes.

Rocket & Grilled Goat's Cheese Salad

INGREDIENTS

30ml/2 tbsp olive oil
30ml/2 tbsp vegetable oil
8 slices of French bread
generous handful of rocket leaves, torn
225g/8oz curly endive, torn
2 x 225g/8oz/2 cups cylindrical chèvre (goat's milk cheeses)
ground black pepper
DRESSING
90ml/6 tbsp walnut oil
30ml/2 tbsp lemon juice
SAUCE
90ml/6 tbsp apricot jam
120ml/4fl oz/½ cup white wine
10ml/2 tsp Dijon mustard

SERVES 4

1 Heat the olive oil and vegetable oil in a large frying pan. Fry the slices of French bread on one side only until pale gold. Lift out with a fish slice and drain on kitchen paper. Make the dressing by whisking the walnut oil and lemon juice together in a small bowl.

2 Make the sauce. Warm the jam in a small saucepan, then press it through a sieve into a clean pan. Stir in the white wine and mustard. Heat gently and keep warm until needed.

3 Toss the rocket and curly endive with the dressing until the leaves are well coated. Arrange on four individual serving plates. Preheat the grill.

4 Cut the goat's cheeses into eight rounds and place one round on the uncooked side of each piece of bread. Grill until the cheese melts, then arrange two croutes on each salad and grind some pepper on top. Serve at once, with the warm apricot sauce.

Roquefort & Walnut Pasta Salad

Ingredients

225g/8oz/2 cups dried pasta shapes
selection of salad leaves (rocket, frisée, lamb's lettuce, baby spinach leaves, radicchio)
30ml/2 tbsp walnut oil
60ml/4 tbsp sunflower oil
30ml/2 tbsp red wine vinegar
225g/8oz/1⅓ cups Roquefort, crumbled
115g/4oz/1 cup walnut halves
salt and ground black pepper

Serves 4

1 Bring a large saucepan of lightly salted water to the boil. Add the pasta and cook for about 10 minutes or according to the instructions on the packet, until just tender. Drain well, rinse under cold water and drain again.

2 Place the salad leaves in a large bowl. Make the dressing by whisking the walnut oil, sunflower oil and red wine vinegar in a small bowl. Add salt and freshly ground black pepper to taste.

3 Tip the pasta into the centre of the salad leaves, and scatter the crumbled Roquefort cheese over the top. Top the salad with the walnut halves and serve with the dressing on the side, ready to be tossed at the table.

Cook's Tip

Toast the walnuts under the grill for a couple of minutes before adding them to the salad, to release their flavour.

Mozzarella, Tomato & Basil Salad

INGREDIENTS

4 large tomatoes
225g/8oz/2 cups mozzarella cheese
8–10 fresh basil leaves
60ml/4 tbsp extra virgin olive oil
salt and freshly ground black pepper

SERVES 4

1 Wash the tomatoes under cold running water and remove the stalks. Using a sharp knife, slice the tomatoes and the mozzarella cheese into thick rounds.

2 Next, arrange the tomatoes and mozzarella in overlapping slices on a large dish. Place a basil leaf behind each tomato slice. Drizzle the olive oil over the salad and sprinkle with a little salt. Serve the salad with the black pepper passed separately.

COOK'S TIP

In Italy the most sought-after mozzarella is made from the milk of water buffalo, but cow's milk mozzarella works equally well.

Desserts

Grilled Nectarines with Ricotta & Spice

INGREDIENTS

4 ripe nectarines or peaches
115g/4oz/½ cup ricotta cheese or fromage frais
15ml/1 tbsp light muscovado sugar
2.5ml/½ tsp ground star anise or mixed spice

SERVES 4

1 Wash the nectarines or peaches, cut them in half and carefully remove the stones. Arrange the fruit, cut-side up, in an ovenproof dish or on a baking sheet.

2 Preheat the grill. Tip the ricotta or fromage frais into a bowl and stir in the sugar. Use a teaspoon to divide the mixture between the hollows in the fruit halves.

3 Sprinkle the fruit with star anise or mixed spice. Grill the nectarines or peaches for 6–8 minutes or until they are hot and the filling is bubbling. Do not place them too close to the heat. Transfer the fruit to dessert plates and serve warm.

Raspberry Vacherin

INGREDIENTS

3 egg whites
175g/6oz/¾ cup caster sugar
15ml/1 tbsp finely chopped almonds
icing sugar, for dusting
raspberries (with leaves, if possible) to decorate

FILLING

175g/6oz/¾ cup low fat soft cheese
15–30ml/1–2 tbsp clear honey
15ml/1 tbsp Cointreau
120ml/4fl oz/½ cup whipped cream or fromage frais
225g/8oz fresh raspberries

SERVES 6

1 Preheat the oven to 140°C/275°F/Gas 1. Draw a 20cm/8in circle on each of two pieces of non-stick baking paper. Turn the paper over and line two large baking sheets.

2 Whisk the egg whites in a grease-free bowl until they are very stiff, then gradually whisk in the caster sugar to make a stiff meringue mixture. Spoon the mixture on to the marked circles on the paper-lined sheets, spreading it evenly to the edges. Sprinkle the chopped almonds over one of the meringue rounds.

3 Bake the meringue rounds for 1½–2 hours, until crisp and golden, then carefully lift them off the paper and allow them to cool on wire racks. Make the filling by creaming the cheese with the honey and liqueur in a bowl. Fold in the whipped cream or fromage frais, then add the raspberries.

4 Place the plain meringue round on a board, spread with the filling and top with the nut-covered meringue. Dust lightly with the icing sugar, then carefully transfer to a serving plate. Decorate with the fresh raspberries and leaves (if available).

COOK'S TIP

For successful meringues, use eggs at room temperature and whisk them until they are so stiff that you can turn the bowl upside-down without the egg whites falling out.

Cheese & Coconut Dumplings with Apricot Sauce

INGREDIENTS

75g/3oz/6 tbsp cottage or curd cheese
1 egg white
30ml/2 tbsp butter
15ml/1 tbsp soft light brown sugar
30ml/2 tbsp self-raising wholemeal flour
finely grated rind of ½ lemon
30ml/2 tbsp toasted shredded coconut, plus extra for sprinkling
SAUCE
225g/8oz can apricots in natural juice
15ml/1 tbsp lemon juice

SERVES 4

1 Fill a steamer halfway with boiling water. Bring the water back to the boil. If you do not have a steamer, place a large heatproof plate over a saucepan of boiling water.

2 Beat the cottage or curd cheese together with the egg white and butter in a large bowl, then stir in the sugar, flour, lemon rind and measured coconut, mixing evenly to a fairly firm dough.

3 Place 12 spoonfuls of the mixture in the steamer or on the plate, leaving a space between them. Cover the steamer or plate tightly, with a lid or a second plate. Steam the dumplings for 10 minutes or until they have risen and are firm to the touch.

4 Meanwhile, purée the apricots with their juice in a blender or food processor. Stir in the lemon juice. Pour into a small pan and heat until boiling. Pour a pool on to each dessert plate, top with three dumplings and sprinkle the extra coconut on top. Serve at once.

Baked Blackberry Cheesecake

INGREDIENTS

175g/6oz/¾ cup cottage cheese
150ml/¼ pint/⅔ cup natural yogurt
15ml/1 tbsp wholemeal flour
30ml/2 tbsp soft light brown sugar
1 egg, plus 1 egg white
finely grated rind and juice of ½ lemon
350g/12oz/2 cups fresh blackberries, hulled

SERVES 4

1 Preheat the oven to 180°C/350°F/Gas 4. Lightly grease and base line an 18cm/7in round cake tin. Process the cottage cheese in a food processor or using a blender until smooth and creamy.

2 Scrape the cheese into a large bowl and stir in the yogurt, flour, sugar, whole egg and egg white. Mix well, then stir in the lemon rind and juice, with most of the blackberries. Save the rest of the blackberries for the decoration.

3 Tip the mixture into the prepared tin and level the surface. Bake for 30–35 minutes, or until just set. Turn off the oven and leave to rest for 30 minutes.

4 Run a sharp knife around the edge of the cheesecake and turn it out. Lift off the lining paper carefully. Place the cheesecake on a serving plate and decorate with the reserved blackberries.

VARIATION

Any other soft berry fruits, such as raspberries or blackcurrants, may be used for the cheesecake, if blackberries are not available.

Walnut & Ricotta Cake

INGREDIENTS

115g/4oz/1 cup walnut pieces
150g/5oz/⅔ cup butter, softened
150g/5oz/⅔ cup caster sugar
5 eggs, separated
finely grated rind of 1 orange
150g/5oz/⅔ cup ricotta cheese
40g/1½ oz/6 tbsp plain flour
TOPPING
60ml/4 tbsp apricot jam
15ml/1 tbsp water
30ml/2 tbsp brandy
50g/2oz bitter or plain chocolate, coarsely grated

SERVES 8

1 Preheat the oven to 190°C/375°F/Gas 5. Grease and base-line a deep 23cm/9in round, loose-based cake tin. Chop the walnuts roughly, then toast them lightly under the grill.

2 In a mixing bowl, cream the butter with 115g/4oz/½ cup of the caster sugar until light and fluffy. Add the egg yolks, orange rind, ricotta, flour and walnuts and mix well.

3 Whisk the egg whites in a grease-free bowl until stiff peaks form. Gradually whisk in the remaining caster sugar. Use a large metal spoon to stir a quarter of the whisked whites into the ricotta mixture to lighten it, then carefully fold in the rest.

4 Spoon the mixture into the prepared tin and level the surface. Bake for about 30 minutes or until the cake has risen and is firm. Leave to cool in the tin.

5 Transfer the cake to a serving plate. Heat the apricot jam with the water in a small pan, then press through a sieve into a jug. Stir in the brandy. Brush the apricot sauce over the cake so that it trickles down the sides. Scatter the top generously with the grated chocolate.

Index